Durga
Chalisa

Published in Sanskriti Press
by Rupa Publications India Pvt. Ltd 2025
7/16, Ansari Road, Daryaganj
New Delhi 110002

Sales centres:
Bengaluru Chennai
Hyderabad Jaipur Kathmandu
Kolkata Mumbai Prayagraj

Edition copyright © Rupa Publications India Pvt. Ltd 2025

All rights reserved.
No part of this publication may be reproduced, transmitted,
or stored in a retrieval system, in any form or by any means,
electronic, mechanical, photocopying, recording or otherwise,
without the prior permission of the publisher.

P-ISBN: 978-93-5702-619-2

First impression 2025

10 9 8 7 6 5 4 3 2 1

Printed in India

This book is sold subject to the condition that it shall not, by way of
trade or otherwise, be lent, resold, hired out, or otherwise circulated,
without the publisher's prior consent, in any form of binding or cover
other than that in which it is published.

Introduction

The **Durga Chalisa** is a revered devotional hymn dedicated to **Goddess Durga**, one of the most powerful and widely worshiped deities in Hinduism. Composed of **forty verses** (hence the name "Chalisa"), the hymn serves as a medium for devotees to express their devotion, seek blessings, and invoke the divine energy of **Maa Durga**. Rooted in ancient tradition, the Durga Chalisa encapsulates the essence of the goddess's valor, compassion, and the divine attributes that make her the ultimate source of strength and protection. The hymn opens with praises to Goddess Durga, acknowledging her as the divine mother who embodies **Shakti**, the supreme energy of the universe, and is capable of destroying evil forces. Each verse poetically describes her various forms, her weapons, and the significance of her appearance, portraying her as both a protector and a destroyer of demons. The Durga Chalisa also recounts mythological tales, such as her victory over the demon **Mahishasura**, highlighting her role in protecting righteousness and upholding justice.

Reciting the Durga Chalisa is believed to invoke the goddess's divine blessings and protection. It fosters inner strength and peace, dispels negativity, and removes obstacles in the lives of devotees. The hymn's verses are infused with energy that encourages self-belief and resilience, and it is especially significant during the festival of **Navratri**, when devotees engage in rituals and prayers to honor Goddess Durga. Through its regular recitation, individuals seek blessings for courage, wisdom, prosperity, and spiritual growth.

Devotees recite the Durga Chalisa as part of their daily prayers or during special occasions. It is often chanted after lighting a **diya** (lamp) and offering flowers, symbolizing devotion and reverence to the goddess. Some prefer reciting the hymn in a meditative state, focusing on the meaning of the verses to enhance their spiritual connection. Group recitations, particularly in temples or during community gatherings, amplify the collective spiritual energy, fostering a sense of unity and devotion.

The **Durga Chalisa** is not merely a prayer; it is a profound reminder of the strength and resilience that lies within each devotee. By embodying the qualities of the goddess—fearlessness, compassion, and power—devotees can navigate life's challenges with grace and determination.

Whether recited for solace, protection, or strength, the Durga Chalisa continues to inspire millions, bridging the divine and the devotee, and serving as a powerful spiritual practice that connects individuals with the goddess's divine blessings.

1

नमो नमो दुर्गे सुख करणि ।
नमो नमो अम्बे दुख हरनि ॥

Namo namo Durge sukh karani |
Namo namo Ambe dukh harani ||

I bow to Goddess Durga, the giver of happiness, and to Goddess Amba, the remover of all sorrows.

2

निरंकार है ज्योति तुम्हारी ।
तिहुँ लोक फैलि उजियारी ।।

Nirankar hai jyoti tumhari |
Tihun lok pheli ujayari ||

You are formless and your divine light spreads across the three worlds, bringing brightness and illumination.

3

शशि ललाट मुख महा विशाल ।
नेत्र लाल बृकुटि विक्राल ।।

Shashi lalat mukh maha vishala |
Netra lal brikuti vikrala ||

Your face is as radiant as the moon, your eyes are red and fierce with an intense gaze.

4

रूप मतु को अधिक सुहावे ।
दर्शन करत जन अति सुख पावे ।।

Roop matu ko adhika suhave |
Daras karat jan ati sukh pave ||

Your form is exceedingly beautiful, and the devotees who witness your divine form attain immense joy.

5

तुम संसार शक्ति लै कीना ।
पालन हेतु अन्न धन दीना ।।

Tum sansar shakti laya kina |
Palan hetu anna dhan dina ||

You are the power of the universe, providing food and wealth for the sustenance of life.

6

अन्नपूर्णा हुई जग पाला ।
तुम्ही आदि सुन्दरी बाला ।।

Annapurna hui jag pala |
Tumhi adi sundari bala ||

You are the embodiment of Annapurna, the nurturer of the world, and you are the eternal and original source of beauty.

7

प्रलय काल सब नाशन हरी ।
तुम गौरी शिव शंकर प्यारी ।।

Pralaya kal sab nashan hari |
Tum Gauri Shiv Shankar pyari ||

During the time of destruction, you are the one who protects, and you are beloved to Lord Shiva.

8

शिव योगी तुम्हारे गुण गावें ।
ब्रह्मा विष्णु तुम्हे नित ध्यानें ॥

Shiv yogi tumhare gun gave |
Brahma Vishnu tumhe nit dhyaven ||

Shiva and yogis praise your qualities, and Brahma and Vishnu constantly meditate upon you.

9

रूप सरस्वती को तुम धारा ।
दे सुविधि ऋषि मुनिन उबार ॥

Roop Saraswati ko tum dhara |
De subudhi rishi munin ubara ||

You are the embodiment of Goddess Saraswati, who provides wisdom and enlightenment to sages and saints.

10

धार्यो रूप नरसिंह को अम्बा ।
प्रगट भयिन फर कर कंबा ॥

Dharyo roop Narsimha ko Amba |
Pragat bhayin phar kar kamba ||

You took the form of Narasimha to protect Prahlada, manifesting in the form of a lion-headed deity.

11

रक्षा करी प्रहलाद बचायो ।
हिरण्यकशिपु को स्वर्ग पठायो ॥

Raksha kari Prahalad bachayo |
Hiranakush ko swarg pathayo ||

You protected Prahlada and sent the demon Hiranyakashipu to heaven.

12

लक्ष्मी रूप धर जग माहीं ।
श्री नारायण अंग समाही ।।

Lakshmii roop dharo jag mahi |
Shree Narayan ang samahi ||

You manifested as Goddess Lakshmi, and you are united with Lord Narayana in the universe.

13

क्षीरसिन्धु में करत विलासा ।
दयासिन्धु दीजै मन आसा ॥

Ksheree Sindhu karat vilasa |
Daya Sindhu deejay man aasa ||

You live in the ocean of milk, and you are the ocean of mercy, fulfilling the desires of the devotees.

14

हिंगलाज में तुमही भवानी ।
महिमा अमित ना जात बखानी ।।

Hingalaj mein tumhi Bhavani |
Mahima amit na jaat bakhani ||

You reside in Hinglaj as Bhavani, and your glory cannot be fully described.

15

मतंगी धूमावती माता ।
भुवनेश्वरी बगला सुखदाता ॥

Matangi Dhoomavati Mata |
Bhuvneshwari Bagala Sukhdata ||

You manifest as Matangi, Dhoomavati, and Bhuvneshwari, bestowing comfort and joy.

16

श्री बैरव तारा योग तारणी ।
छिन्न भाल भव दु:ख निवारिण ॥

Shree Bairav Tara jog tarani |
Chinna Bhala bhav dukh nivarani ||

You are the protector in the form of Bhairav, saving the devotees from sorrow.

17

केहरी वाहन सोह भवानी ।
लंगूर वीर चलत अग्रवानी ।।

Keheri Vahan soh Bhavani |
Langur veer chalat agavani ||

You travel on a lion's vehicle, and you are protected by a courageous monkey army.

18

कर में खप्पर खडग विराजे ।
जाको देख काल डर भागे ॥

Kar men khappar khadag viraje |
Jako dekh kal dar bhaje ||

In your hand, you hold a skull cup and a sword, and seeing you, even time (Kala) fears.

19

सोहे अस्त्र और त्रिशूल ।
जैसे उठाता शत्रु हिया शूल ॥

Sohe astra aur trishoola |
Jaise uthata shatru hiya shoola ||

You bear a divine weapon and trident, which pierces the hearts of your enemies.

20

नागर्कोट में तुमही विराजत ।
तिहुँ लोक में डंका बजत ॥

Nagarkot mein tumhi virajat |
Tihun lok mein danka bajat ||

You reside in the city of Nagarkot, and your divine glory echoes across the three worlds.

21

शम्भु निषम्भु दानुज तुम मारे ।
रक्तबीज शंखन संहारे ॥

Shumbhu Nishumbhu Danuja tum mare |
Rakta-beeja shankhan samhare ||

You defeated demons like Shumbhu and Nishumbhu, and you destroyed the Raktabeeja demon.

22

महिषासुर नृप अति अभिमानी ।
जेही अग्रह भर माही अकुलानी ॥

Mahishasur nripa ati abhimani |
Jehi agha bhar mahi akulani ||

You slayed the arrogant and powerful demon Mahishasura, bringing peace to the world.

23

रूप कालराल कालीक धारा ।
सेन सहित तुम तीन संहार ॥

Roop kaaral Kalika dhara |
Sen sahita tum tin samhara ||

You take the form of Kali, destroying demons along with your army.

24

परी भीड़ संतन पर जब-जब ।
भयि सहाया मातु तुम तब तब ॥

Pari garha santan par jab jab |
Bhayi sahaya Matu tum tab tab ||

Whenever the saints or children face difficulties, you are always there to help them.

25

अमरपुरी अरु बसावा लोक ।
तव महिमा सब रहें शोक ।।

Amarpuri aru basava loka |
Tava mahima sab rahen asoka ||

In the divine realms and all worlds, your glory brings peace and joy.

26

ज्वाला में है ज्योति तुम्हारी ।
तुम्हें सदा पूजन नर-नारी ॥

Jwala mein hai jyoti tumhari |
Tumhen sada pujan nar nari ||

Your light burns in the flame, and all humans worship you constantly.

27

प्रेम भक्ति से जो यश गाए ।
दुःख दरिद्र निकट नहीं आए ।।

Prem bhakti se jo yash gaye |
Dukh daridra nikat nahin aaye ||

Those who chant your glory with love and devotion are free from sorrow and poverty.

28

ध्यान करें तुमें जो नर मन लाए ।
जनम-मरण ताको छुटी जाए ।।

Dhyave tumhen jo nar man laee |
Janam-maran tako chuti jaee ||

Whoever meditates on you with a pure heart, is freed from the cycle of birth and death.

29

योगी सुर-मुनि कहत पुकारे ।
योग न हो बिन शक्ति तुम्हारी ॥

Yogi sur-muni kahat pukari |
Jog na ho bin shakti tumhari ||

All yogis and sages proclaim that yoga cannot be attained without your divine power.

30

शंकर आचारज तप कीन्हो ।
काम क्रोध जीत सब लीन्हो ।।

Shankar Aacharaj tap keenhon |
Kam krodh jeet sab leenhon ||

Shankar (Lord Shiva) performed extreme penance, overcoming desires and anger with your grace.

31

निषिद्धिन ध्यान धरो शंकर को ।
काहू काल नहीं सुमिरन तुम को ।।

Nisidhin dhyan dharo Shanker ko |
Kahu kal nahin sumiron tum ko ||

One who meditates on Lord Shiva does not experience fear, as long as they remember you.

32

शक्ति रूप को मरम न पायो ।
शक्ति गई तब मन पछितायो ।।

Shakti roop ko maram na payo |
Shakti gayi tab man pachitayo ||

When the essence of your power is lost, the mind regrets, for your power is the ultimate truth.

33

शरणागत हुई कीर्ति बखानी ।
जय जय जय जगदंब भवानी ।।

Sharnagat hui keerti bakhani |
Jai jai jai Jagdamb Bhavani ||

The one who takes refuge in you finds glory, and praises your name in all ways.

34

भयी प्रसन्ना आदि जगदंबा ।
दयी शक्ति नहीं कीन विलम्बा ॥

Bhayi prasanna Aadi Jagdamba |
Dayi shakti nahin keen vilamba ||

You are the original goddess, who grants power and mercy without delay.

35

मोको माटु कष्ट अतिगेरो ।
तुम बिन कौन हरे दुःख मेरो ॥

Mokun Matu kashta ati ghero |
Tum bin kaun hare dukh mero ||

Oh Mother, in times of great suffering, who else but you can relieve my pain?

36

आशा तृष्णा निपत सतावें ।
मोह मदादिक सब बिनसावें ।।

Asha trishna nipat sataven |
Moh madadik sab binsaven ||

You end the desires and illusions, freeing the soul from them.

37

शत्रु नाश कीजै महारानी ।
सुमिरन एकचित तुमीमद भवानी ॥

Shatru nash keeje Maharani |
Sumiron ekachita tumhen Bhavani ||

O Queen, destroy my enemies and let me remember you with a single mind.

38

करो कृपा हे मातु दयाला ।
ऋद्धि-सिद्धि दे करूण हलाला ॥

Karo kripa hey Matu dayala |
Riddhi-Siddhi de karahu nihala ||

Show your kindness and grant me success and wisdom.

39

जब लगि जिऊं दया फल पाऊँ ।
तुम्हरो यश मैं सदा सुनाऊँ ॥

Jab lagi jiyoon daya phal paoon |
Tumro yash mein sada sunaoon ||

As long as I live, may I always sing your praise and receive the fruits of your mercy.

40

दुर्गा चालिसा जो गए ।
सब सुख भोग परंपद पावे ।।

Durga chalisa jo gaye |
Sab sukh bhog parampad pave ||

Anyone who recites this Durga Chalisa attains happiness and reaches the highest realm.

देवदास शरण निज जानी ।
करहु कृपा जगदंब भवानी ॥

Devidas sharan nij jani |
Karahu kripa Jagdamb Bhavani ||

I, Devidas, take refuge in you, O Jagdamba, and request your blessings.

इति श्री दुर्गा चालीसा सम्पूर्णम् ।।

Iti Sri Durga Chalisa Sampurnam ||

Thus ends the Durga Chalisa.

दुर्गा आरती

जय अम्बे गौरी, मैया जय श्यामा गौरी।
तुमको निशदिन ध्यावत, हरि ब्रह्मा शिवरी।।
ॐ जय अम्बे.....

मांग सिंदूर बिराजत, टीको मृगमद को।
उज्ज्वल से दोउ नैना, चंद्रबदन नीको।।
ॐ जय अम्बे.....

कनक समान कलेवर, रक्ताम्बर राजै।
रक्तपुष्प गल माला, कंठन पर साजै।।
ॐ जय अम्बे.....

केहरि वाहन राजत, खड्ग खप्परधारी।
सुर-नर मुनिजन सेवत, तिनके दुःखहारी।।
ॐ जय अम्बे.....

कानन कुण्डल शोभित, नासाग्रे मोती।
कोटिक चंद्र दिवाकर, राजत समज्योति।।
ॐ जय अम्बे.....

शुम्भ निशुम्भ बिडारे, महिषासुर घाती।
धूम्र विलोचन नैना, निशिदिन मदमाती।।
ॐ जय अम्बे.....

चण्ड-मुण्ड संहारे, शौणित बीज हरे।
मधु कैटभ दोउ मारे, सुर भयहीन करे।।
ॐ जय अम्बे.....

ब्रह्माणी, रुद्राणी, तुम कमला रानी।
आगम निगम बखानी, तुम शिव पटरानी।।
ॐ जय अम्बे.....

चौंसठ योगिनि मंगल गावैं, नृत्य करत भैरू।
बाजत ताल मृदंगा, अरू बाजत डमरू।।
ॐ जय अम्बे.....

तुम ही जग की माता, तुम ही हो भरता।
भक्तन की दुःख हरता, सुख सम्पत्ति करता।।
ॐ जय अम्बे.....

भुजा चार अति शोभित, खड्ग खप्परधारी।
मनवांछित फल पावत, सेवत नर नारी।।
ॐ जय अम्बे.....

कंचन थाल विराजत, अगर कपूर बाती।
श्री मालकेतु में राजत, कोटि रतन ज्योति।।
ॐ जय अम्बे.....

अम्बेजी की आरती जो कोई नर गावै।
कहत शिवानंद स्वामी, सुख-सम्पत्ति पावै।।
ॐ जय अम्बे.....

Durga Aarti

Jay Ambe Gauri, Maiya Jay Shyama Gauri.
Tumko Nishdin Dhyaavat, Hari Brahma Shivri.
Om Jay Ambe...

Maang Sindoor Birajat, Teeko Mrigmad Ko.
Ujjwal Se Dou Naina, Chandrabadan Neeko.
Om Jay Ambe...

Kanak Samaam Kalevar, Raktambar Raajai.
Raktpushp Gal Mala, Kanthan Par Saajai.
Om Jay Ambe...

Keheri Vahan Raajat, Khadg Khappardhari.
Sur-Nar Munijan Sevat, Tinke Dukhhaari.
Om Jay Ambe...

Kanan Kundal Shobhith, Nasagre Moti.
Kotik Chandra Divakar, Raajat Samajyoti.
Om Jay Ambe...

Shumbh Nishumbh Bidare, Mahishasur Ghati.
Dhoomra Velochan Naina, Nishidin Madamaati.
Om Jay Ambe...

Chand-Mund Sanhare, Shaunit Beej Hare.
Madhukaitabh Douv Maare, Sur Bhayheen Kare.
Om Jay Ambe...

Brahmani, Rudrani, Tum Kamala Rani.
Aagam Nigam Bakhani, Tum Shiv Patraani.
Om Jay Ambe...

Chaunsath Yogini Mangal Gaavain, Nritya Karat Bhairu.
Bajat Taal Mridanga, Aru Bajat Damru.
Om Jay Ambe...

Tum Hi Jag Ki Mata, Tum Hi Ho Bharta.
Bhaktan Ki Dukh Harata, Sukh Sampatti Karta.
Om Jay Ambe...

Bhuja Char Ati Shobhith, Khadg Khappardhari.
Manwanchhit Phal Paavat, Sevat Nar Nari.
Om Jay Ambe...

Kanchan Thaal Virajat, Agar Kapoor Baati.
Shri Malketu Mein Rajat, Koti Ratan Jyoti.
Om Jay Ambe...

Ambeji Ki Aarti Jo Koi Nar Gaave.
Kahat Shivanand Swami, Sukh-Sampatti Paave.
Om Jay Ambe...

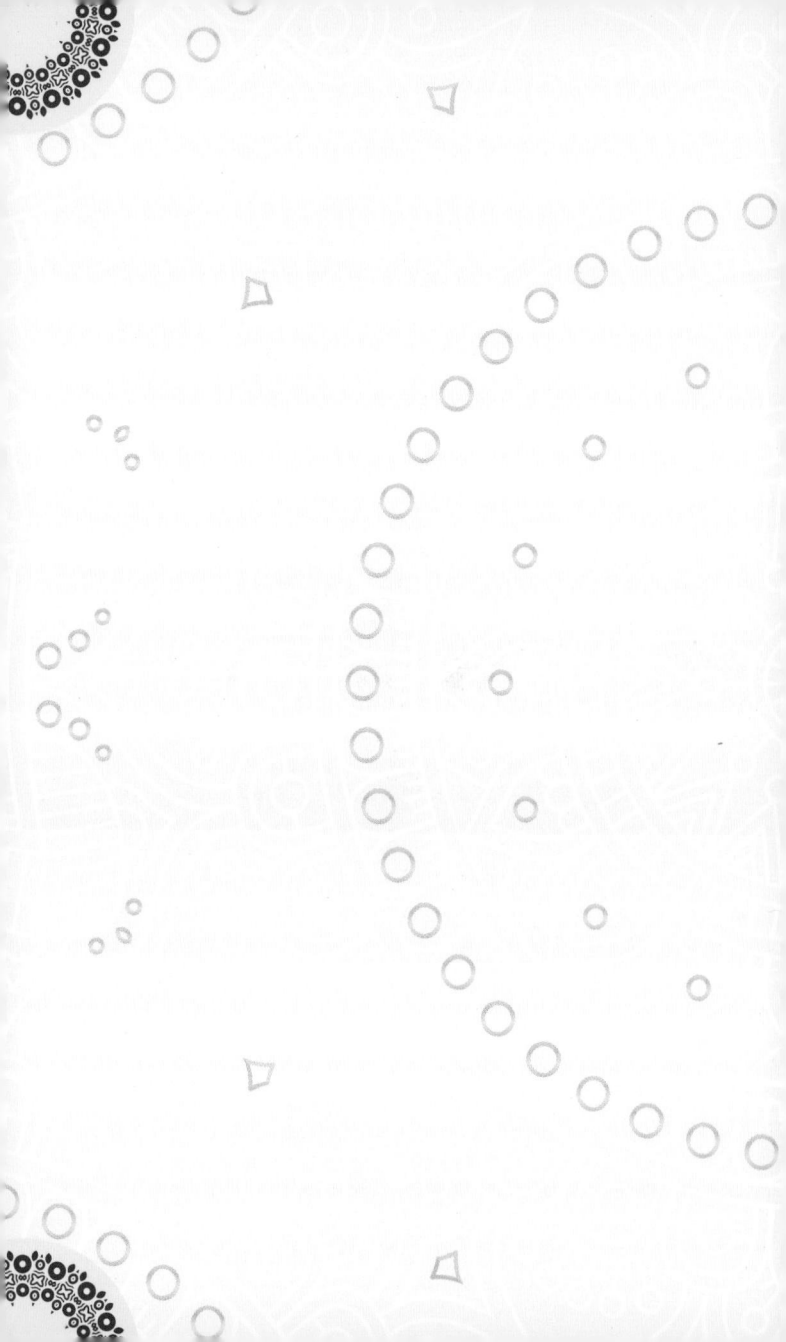